Happy Trails

Bloom County Books by Berke Breathed

Loose Tails

'Toons for Our Times

Penguin Dreams and Stranger Things

Bloom County Babylon: Five Years of Basic Naughtiness

Billy and the Boingers Bootleg

Tales Too Ticklish to Tell

The Night of the Mary Kay Commandos

Happy Trails

Happy Trails

Berke Breathed

A Bloom County Book

Little, Brown and Company • Boston Toronto London

First Edition

Library of Congress Cataloging-in-Publication Data

Breathed, Berke.
   [Bloom County. Selections]
   Happy Trails / Berke Breathed. — 1st ed.
     p.   cm.
   Selections from the author's comic strip, Bloom County.
   "A Bloom County book."
   ISBN 0-316-10741-7
   I. Title.   II. Title: Bloom County.
PN6728.B57B72   1990
741.5'973 — dc20   89-29865
                                             CIP

10 9 8 7 6 5 4 3 2 1

RAI

Designed by Barbara Werden

Published simultaneously in Canada by
Little, Brown & Company (Canada) Limited

Printed in the United States of America

Critic's Page

"I never thought Berke Breathed had talent,
so he was probably forced to quit."

DONALD TRUMP
Albany, New York
May 4, 1989

Happy Trails

1

TODAY'S
MEDICAL
SPECIAL:

**LIPOSUCTION
EXPLAINED**

FOR
LATER
REFERENCE

Clip 'N' Save!

WHAT IS IT?
LIPOSUCTION IS THE
"VACUUMING" OF UNWANTED
FAT CELLS FROM PARTS
OF THE BODY IN NEED
OF SLIMMING.

EPIDERMIS
SLURP!!
FAT CELLS

WHERE DOES ONE
GET IT?
YOUR LOCAL, LEGAL
LIPOSUCTION
CLINIC.

The
HOOVER
LIPO
CLINIC

WHO HAS IT DONE?
ANY INDIVIDUAL WITH
A LOCALIZED WEIGHT
PROBLEM.

PROBLEM
AREA

HOLD MY CALLS, PLEASE.
I'M OFF TO HAVE MY
NOSE LIPOSUCTIONED.

YOU
HAVEN'T
HEARD?

HEARD
WHAT?

THE SUPREME COURT
RULED IT UNCONSTITU-
TIONAL LAST WEEK...
AND YOU KNOW WHAT
THAT
MEANS...

ILLEGAL
BACK-ALLEY
LIPOSUCTIONS.!!

ZIP!

I'M LEAVING
BEFORE THIS GOES
ANYWHERE.

EXCUSE ME...
I'M LOOKING FOR
A CERTAIN
GENTLEMAN...

"GUIDO THE
BACK-ALLEY
LIPOSUCTIONIST."

WHO'S
LOOKIN'
FOR 'IM?

UH...

PROBABLY
THE A.M.A.
**NEVER
MIND.**

C'MERE...

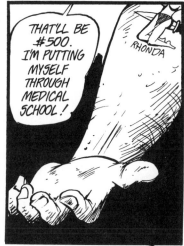

3

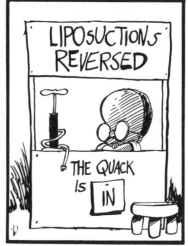

5

6

11

Panel 1: HI, DAD. / GOOD LORD. WHAT HAPPENED TO YOU, SON?

Panel 2: ACID SNOW... OZONE DEPLETION... NUKE LEAKS... THE WHOLE ENCHILADA.

Panel 3: WELL, GO TAKE A HOT BATH. YOU'LL FEEL BETTER.

Panel 4: ENVIRONMENTAL CONSCIOUSNESS MISSES A FOOTHOLD IN THE BINKLEY HOUSEHOLD. / SON, I KNOW YOUR BRAIN'S TURNED INTO A SLURPEE BUT DON'T FORGET YOUR HOMEWORK.

Panel 5: I DUNNO...

Panel 6: SEEMS LIKE THINGS ARE GETTIN' WORSE QUICKER THAN THEY'RE GETTIN' BETTER. / ACID SNOW

Panel 7: AH... LOOK WHO'S AT THE BEACH!...

Panel 8: KIDS, DON'T TRY THIS AT HOME. / ACME HOSPITAL WASTE / BEACH IN JAN.? GLOBAL WARMING?

Panel 9: HOUSE-CLEANING TIME!

Panel 10: ..OR RATHER, CLOSET-CLEANING. WE'VE FOUND SOME LEFTOVERS FROM LAST YEAR:

Panel 11: LEONA HELMSLEY, REV. AL SHARPTON, ROBIN GIVENS AAAND... SIX MILLION OLLIE NORTH HAIRCUTS.

Panel 12: CALL "GOODWILL." / I THOUGHT WE'D JUST PUT 'EM IN YOUR BED.

13

14

CLIP 'N' SAVE

16

17

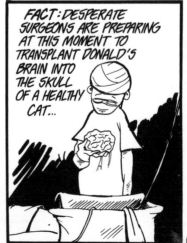
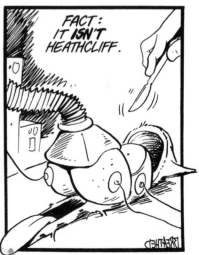

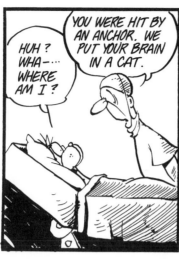

19

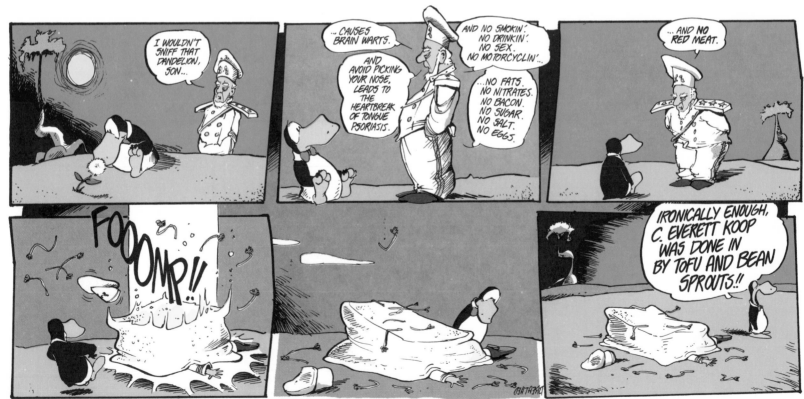

20

21

I'D LIKE TO APOLOGIZE FOR YESTERDAY'S WHOLLY UNSANCTIONED SATIRICAL ATTACK ON THE VICE-PRESIDENT'S LOVELY WIFE.

W.A. THORNHUMP C.E.O., BLOOM COUNTY, INC.

BAD PENGUIN! BAD, BAD PENGUIN! NAUGHTY PENGUIN!!

OBVIOUSLY, HE WAS UNAWARE THAT THE CARTOON TAX BILL IS UP FOR PRESIDENTIAL VETO THIS WEEK... HA! HA!

WHO AM I? MARILYN QUAYLE OR MARY TYLER MOORE IN 1962?

BAD PENGUIN! IMPOLITIC PENGUIN!

DON'T HANG UP ON ME AGAIN, IVANA! IT'S ME... YOUR DONALD!

THAT'S RIGHT... I'M A PENNILESS CAT NOW... BUT I'M STILL ME!...

LESS ABOUT $600 MILLION.

... AREN'T I JUST AS LOVABLE A GUY WITHOUT THE $600 MIL?!

OR IS THAT A STUPID QUESTION?

MUNCH MUNCH CHEW SNORT CHOMP

MOVIE BUFFS: ANY OF THIS LOOK FAMILIAR?

UGH! TURNIPS!... I'VE BEEN FORCED TO EAT TURNIPS TO SURVIVE!...

AS GOD IS IN HEAVEN AND DONALD TRUMP IS MY NAME...

HINT: CLARK GABLE, VIVIEN LEIGH...

...I'LL NEVER BE POOR AGAIN!

NO, NOT "FLUBBER."

23

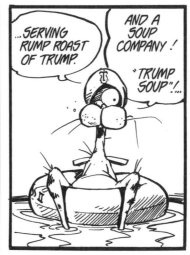

24

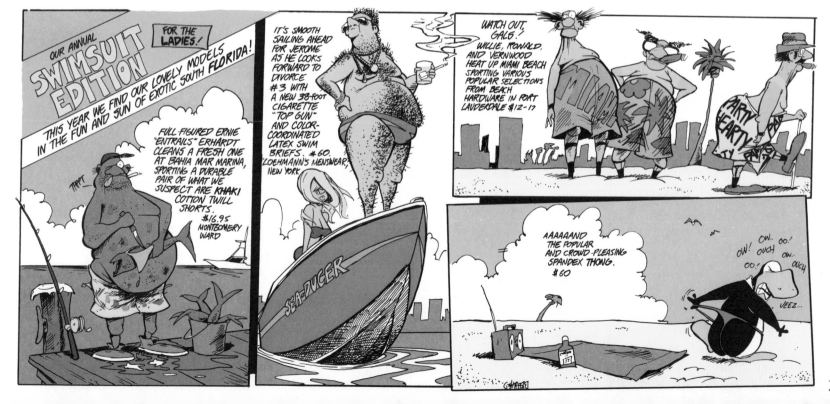

26

27

TODAY, IN A DRAMATIC CAP TO "**NUDENESS WEEK**," OPUS VISITS THE 'ACME STEWARDESS SCHOOL.'

HOWEVER... FOR THE BENEFIT OF THE FEW **COWARDLY** LOCAL EDITORS AMONG OUR CLIENTS, THIS ALTERNATE STRIP FEATURING A **NUDE DONALD TRUMP** HAS BEEN OFFERED AS A WIMPY AND PRUDISH OPTION.

IF YOU'RE READING THESE WORDS, YOU NOW KNOW WHAT SORT OF PRIGGISH BLUENOSES RUN THIS NEWSPAPER.

NOT A STEWARDESS

YA KNOW, BOY... I'M A DEEPLY PHILOSOPHICAL MAN...

OF COURSE, MR. TRUMP.

WHILE I WAS NUDE THIS WEEK... STRIPPED OF ALL PRETENSE... I COULD SEE THAT DEEP DOWN, YOU... ME... EVERYBODY...

...WE'RE ALL THE SAME PERSON.

A RUBE WITH TOO MUCH LOOT?

YES... _NO!_

AAIGH!

ARGH!! YA YEE! YEE! YEE!

SORRY, OL' BOY. WE WERE DOING A LITTLE PRIMAL-SCREAM THERAPY.

IF CATERWAULING COCKROACHES AREN'T ONE OF THE BIBLICAL SIGNS OF THE END OF THE WORLD, THEY _SHOULD BE._

31

WE'VE SOLVED IT. OUR GREAT MINDS ARE ALL AGREED.

THE SCIENTIFIC COMMUNITY NOW KNOWS HOW TIME... REALITY...THE UNIVERSE... **EVERYTHING** BEGAN:

THE BIG BANG.

THE BIG BANG?

THE BIG BANG...

YEAH, BUT WHAT WAS THERE BEFORE—

YESSIR... ...A **REAL** BIG BANG, WE FIGURE.

THAT'S IT? JUST A BIG BOOM?

BANG. THE BIG BANG.

WE FIGURE 352.7 BILLION YEARS AGO, EVERYTHING SUDDENLY EXPLODED INTO BEING. THEN THERE WERE GALAXIES, SUNS AND, AFTER A WHILE, KOALA BEARS.

SOUNDS A LITTLE FLACCID. WHAT WAS AROUND BEFORE THE EXPLOSIO—

IT WAS JUST A BIG BANG! IT'S PERFECTLY LOGICAL! SUBJECT CLOSED!

SCIENTISTS DON'T LIKE BEING STUMPED.

WE'LL HAVE A CURE FOR THE COMMON COLD ANY DAY NOW!!

I'LL TRY TO EXPLAIN THIS IN TERMS THAT THE MOLLUSK-LIKE BRAIN OF THE TYPICAL LAYMAN CAN GRASP:

THE UNIVERSE EXPLODES... SLOWLY EXPANDS...THEN GRAVITY DRAWS IT TOGETHER...IT COLLAPSES... AND **EXPLODES** AGAIN!

A NEVER-ENDING CYCLE... OVER AND OVER... FOREVER REPEATING.

CURIOUSLY, THE IDEA OCCURRED TO STEPHEN HAWKING WHILE WATCHING "I LOVE LUCY."

I KNEW IT!!

FOOOSH!

...AND HERE ON YOUR RIGHT IS THE ENDANGERED "BALD-BOTTOMED, BI-NOSTRILLED EARTHCRITTER"...

CAREFUL, EVERYONE... HE MAY CHARGE!...

...THEY'RE DANGEROUSLY SHORTSIGHTED!

...FACT, AT THE RATE THEY'RE CURDLING THEIR ATMOSPHERE, FLATTENING THEIR FORESTS AND BUILDING STINKING MOUNTAINS OF THOUSAND-YEAR PLASTIC "PAMPERS"...

...THEY'LL BE EXTINCT ANY DAY!

HOWEVER... WE HAVE A BREEDING PROGRAM BACK AT THE ZOO ON ZORT... SO THERE'S STILL HOPE!

CLICK CLICK

FOOM!

HOPE, SHMOPE. YOU REALIZE THEIR BREEDING PAIR ARE ELVIS AND BIGFOOT.

WHERE ARE WE GOING TODAY?

TO THE START OF TIME!

IN A CHAIR?

IT'S THE STEPHEN HAWKING METHOD®... LET'S GO DISCOVER THE TRUE BEGINNING OF THE UNIVERSE!

AT THE NUMBING SPEED OF THOUGHT, OUR MINDS JOURNEY BACKWARD THROUGH SPACE-TIME...

FASTER THAN A YUGO!

STEERING BY OUR INFINITE POWERS OF REASON AND IMAGINATION... WE GO BACK FURTHER...

...AND FURTHER...

...UNTIL WE FINALLY WITNESS THE ACTUAL, ANCIENT SOURCE OF THE COSMOS!

HMM...

POOT!

GRUNT

TRUMP COSMOS FARMS, INC.

ACTUALLY, I'M A LITTLE SURPRISED I ARRIVED AT THAT...

I'M SORRY. THAT WAS ME. YOU STEER NEXT TIME.

44

46

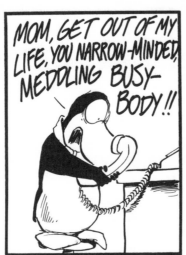

FINALLY REVEALED:

WHAT YOUR COCKROACHES ARE DOING THE SECOND BEFORE YOU TURN ON THE LIGHTS...

(EXCLUSIVE)

CLICK!

SCATTER!

NOW SQUIRT THE "CHEEZ WHIZ" IN THEIR UNDERWEAR!

AT NINE MILES UP, THE MIGHTY SHUTTLE BOOSTERS FALL AWAY...

SUDDENLY... A SYSTEMS ERROR! THE NOSE CONE HAS BROKEN AWAY AND IS HURTLING TOWARD THE EARTH...

STOP THE STORY!

I HAVE A PROBLEM.

IT BETTER BE GOOD.

WHAT'S THE MATTER?

SOMEONE PUT "CHEEZ WHIZ" IN MY SHORTS.

AT NINE MILES UP, THE MIGHTY SHUTTLE BOOSTERS (AGAIN) FALL AWAY...

...SUDDENLY... A SYSTEMS ERROR! THE NOSE CONE HAS BROKEN AWAY AND IS HURTLING TOWARD EARTH!

...WHERE A GENTLE PILGRIM STROLLS INTO HIS FAVORITE SPRING MEADOW...

...AND INTO ETERNITY.

PHEWT!

KIDS! ISN'T THIS MORE EXCITING THAN "GARFIELD"?

OH MY GOSH!

PANT PANT PANT

THERE'S A SIX—NO, TEN-FOOT CUCARACHA IN MY BEDROOM!!

HE HIT ME WITH A LOG AND...AND SCREAMED, "PARDON SPIRO AGNEW!"

ACTUALLY, I SAID "GIMME A 'DING-DONG', HORSEFACE."

HE'S SO POLITICAL!

YAWN

HOLD IT.

WHAT?

YOU GOT SLEEP STUFF IN YOUR EYES.

I'M SO EMBARRASSED.

DON'T BE. THE POPE PROBABLY GETS IT, TOO.

EYE BOOGERS. THE GREAT SOCIAL EQUALIZER.

PEEP! PEEP! PEEP! PEEP!

BOING BOING BOING BOING!

THANK GOD FOR DORK DETECTORS!

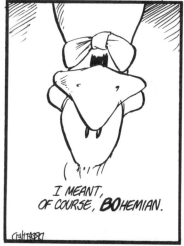

57

THERE! A FALLING STAR! UH... I WISH... I WISH I COULD BE A BALLERINA SOMEDAY!

THERE'S ANOTHER ONE! QUICK, A WISH, OPUS!

I WISH THEY'D STICK OLIVER NORTH IN THE SAME JAIL CELL WITH THE "GODFATHER OF SOUL," JAMES BROWN!

IT HAS ITS OWN PECULIAR APPEAL, DOESN'T IT?

RONALD-ANN!! LOOK! A FALLING STAR!

I WISH... I WISH... UH... WHAT DO I WISH?

I WISH I KNEW IF I'LL HAVE MEANINGFUL EMPLOYMENT AFTER AUGUST 6.

MILO HERE, WITH A "ROSEBUD MATERNITY REPORT."

SHE'S DOING GREAT!... ...GLOWING WITH THE ECSTATIC RAPTURE OF MOTHERHOOD! SEE FOR YOURSELVES!

LIES! PREGNANCY IS A MALE PLOT! CONSPIRED BY MEN TO KEEP US FAT, POWERLESS AND IM-MOBILE! IT'S A PLOT! IT'S

HA! HA! HA! HA! WOMEN AND THEIR NUTTY HORMONES!

58

MEN, TAKE NOTE: PREGNANT GALS GO THROUGH A TEMPORARY PHASE OF INSECURITY ABOUT THEIR APPEARANCE.

THE ANTIDOTE? ...A SUBTLE, SENSITIVE **COMPLIMENT!**

MY! YOU—

DROP DEAD.

I'VE FINISHED MY AUTOBIOGRAPHY.

I'VE INCLUDED EVERY SINGLE SIGNIFICANT THING THAT EVER HAPPENED TO ME.

AND IT'S STILL ONLY 6½ PAGES LONG.

SOME OF US FIND OUR LIVES ABRIDGED EVEN BEFORE THE PAPERBACK COMES OUT.

THIS IS YOUR LIFE STORY?

YUP. EVERYTHING. I THINK IT HAS COMMERCIAL POSSIBILITIES.

ANY SEX?

BEG PARDON?

SEX.

SEX?

ANY IN HERE?

BARRING ANY COPULATING BUGS IN THE BINDING, NO.

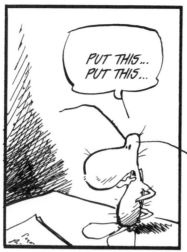

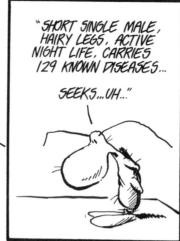

64

LOOK... THE JUNE ISSUE.

WHAT? "LIFE" MAGAZINE?

THE GAL ON THE COVER HAS HER BLOUSE WIDE OPEN.

"HURRAH FOR THE BRA!" IT SAYS.

MORE BLOUSELESS GALS INSIDE...

"IT'S 100 YEARS OLD THIS MONTH: HURRAH FOR THE BRA!"

WOW! WHAT A SCOOP!

MAYBE "NEWSWEEK" HAS "HURRAH FOR HOOTERS!"

IT'S HAPPENING!! ROSEBUD'S HAVING HER BABY!!

WHAT IF THINGS GO WRONG?! WHAT IF ALIENS ATTACK DURING DELIVERY?! WHAT... WHAT...

WAIT... I'M NOT GOING TO PANIC... THE WORLD IS A PLACE OF REASON... EVERYTHING WILL BE FINE... LOGIC RULES HUMAN EVENTS.

OBVIOUSLY HE HASN'T HEARD ABOUT "LIFE"'S SPECIAL BRA ISSUE.

COPIES STILL AVAILABLE!!

I'M ABOUT TO BE A DAD?! NOW?! AN IMMINENT OFFSPRING?!

LESSEE... THE MOTHER'S PART BASSET HOUND... PART ANTELOPE... AND I'M A JACK RABBIT... SO THE KID'S GONNA BE... UH...

... A JACKABASSELOPE.

AAIGH!

THANK GOD MARLIN PERKINS DIDN'T LIVE TO SEE THIS!

AAARGH!

67

I'M WATCHING GARY COLEMAN PLAY OUT MY LIFE IN "NAKED CAME I: THE TV MOVIE."

MILO, WOULD YOU HAVE ANY IDEA HOW THIS ABOMINATION ENDS?

YEAH. HE ENDS UP WATCHING HIS LIFE LIBELED IN FRONT OF MILLIONS, SO HE GRABS A BAZOOKA AND GOES AFTER THE GUY PLAYING ME.

SWEPT HELPLESSLY ALONG BY THE TIDE OF HISTORY!

KIDS! YESTERDAY, YOU SAW ME SITTING **THIS** CLOSE TO THE TELEVISION SCREEN.

DON'T TRY THAT YOURSELVES! AS YOUR PARENTS CAN EXPLAIN, THE FOLLOWING CAN EASILY HAPPEN:

PHEWPPPPPT...

SO BE CAREFUL!

PLUS, DON'T CHASE PEOPLE WITH BAZOOKAS.

PUBLIC SERVICE MESSAGE

STEVE DALLAS HAS MET A GIRL, PORTNOY... I THINK HE'S GONE OFF THE DEEP END.

IN FACT, I...UH...

THEY SHOW "REFORM-SCHOOL VIXENS" ON **HBO** AGAIN LAST NIGHT?

YEAH.

HEY, HONEY...WHOSE GUITAR PICK IS THIS IN YOUR MAKEUP CASE?

BETTER HOMES AND PENGUINS

SOB! I DON'T LOVE HIM! IT WAS JUST PHYSICAL! I WAS WEAK! I'LL END IT TODAY! ...IT BELONGS TO THE BASS PLAYER FOR "GUNS 'N' SPITTLE"...

I'VE BEEN GIVING HIM ALL THE POCKET CHANGE I STEAL FROM YOUR PANTS WHILE YOU SLEEP...PLUS ANY TIPS I EARN FOR "JELL-O WRESTLING" AT VARIOUS BARS AROUND TOWN.

I KNOW YOU'LL UNDERSTAND. YOUR FATHER DOES. HE WRESTLES ME TUESDAYS.

PLEASE DON'T LET THIS AFFECT YOUR BASIC TRUSTING ATTITUDE TOWARD PEOPLE. I LOVED YOU FOR THAT.

ANYWAY... I'M OFF. YOUR MOTHER AND I HAVE A SHIPMENT OF PLASTIC EXPLOSIVES COMING IN.

SMACK!

AS LONG AS WE'RE CLEARING THE AIR, YOU SHOULD KNOW THAT I'VE BEEN COMBING MY NOSE HAIR WITH YOUR TOOTHBRUSH.

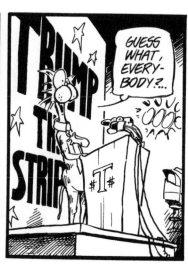

BOYS, THE **GOOD NEWS** IS THAT THE SUN ISN'T DUE TO EXPLODE FOR ANOTHER SIX BILLION YEARS...

...WHALES ARE COMING BACK FROM THE BRINK...

...AND DONNIE OSMOND IS HAVING A BIG COMEBACK.

THE BAD NEWS IS THAT DONALD TRUMP NOW OWNS YOUR LITTLE FANNIES.

STOP IT! EVERYBODY STOP IT! THIS IS UPSETTING ME!!

LIFE'S GETTING TOO WISHY-WASHY!! COMIC STRIPS AREN'T SUPPOSED TO **END**! ..NEITHER ARE GOOD MARRIAGES!

OR FRIENDSHIPS. OR LOYALTIES. OR HAPPINESS... ..HAPPINESS ISN'T SUPPOSED TO JUST END...

GILDA RADNER ISN'T SUPPOSED TO END. PROBABLY THE GOVERNMENT'S FAULT.

JEEZ! PRETTY SLIM PICKINGS!

CARTOON JOBS

STEVE DALLAS WANTS TO APPLY FOR WORK AS A CARTOON SUPERHERO...

HE SEZ ONLY COMIC BOOKS OFFER THE MATURE ENVIRONMENT HE NEEDS AS A LITERATE CARTOON ACTOR...

NOTICE, OPUS, THAT **EVERY** WOMAN IN THESE THINGS LOOKS LIKE DOLLY PARTON IN ZERO GRAVITY! UH-HUH.

"MEN FEAR SOLITUDE AS THEY FEAR SILENCE, BECAUSE BOTH GIVE THEM A GLIMPSE OF THE TERROR OF LIFE'S NOTHINGNESS."
— SOMEBODY

EVERYONE'S LEAVING SOON. I'LL BE ALONE. SILENCE... NOTHINGNESS...

TOTAL BUMMER.

I TOLD YOU I'LL STAY.

YOU WON'T. STEVE SAID THAT TOO, BUT HE'S OFF WORKING IN COMIC BOOKS WITH VOLUPTUOUS, LOOSE WOMEN WITH LITTLE NOSES.

UH... I DON'T THINK HE'S MADE IT THERE QUITE YET.

HMM?

AT LEAST HE'S WORKING. LOOK.

OH, MY.

cathy

I BROUGHT MY TOOTH-BRUSH.

AACK!

OUT! OUT! OUT! NOW!

81

84

86